My Bonus Mom!

Taking the Step out of Stepmom

Steve,
"Mr Angel"
Thank you for
your support!

Tami Butcher

To Steve
Keep Smiling &
Have You _[signature]_

A Division of Five Star Publications, Inc.
Chandler, Arizona

Linda F. Radke, President
Five Star Publications, Inc.
P.O. Box 6698
Chandler, Arizona 85246-6698

www.FiveStarPublications.com
www.MyBonusMomBook.com

Library of Congress Cataloging-in-Publication Data

Butcher, Tami.
 My bonus mom! / by Tami Butcher.
    p. cm.
 Includes bibliographical references and index.
 ISBN-13: 978-1-58985-081-1 (alk. paper)
 ISBN-10: 1-58985-081-5 (alk. paper)
 eISBN: 978-1-58985-082-8
 1. Stepmothers--Juvenile literature. 2. Family relationships--Juvenile
literature. I. Title.
 HQ759.92.B88 2011
 306.874'7--dc23

                        2011019486

Electronic edition provided by
www.eStarPublish.com

the eDivision of Five Star Publications, Inc.
Printed in the United States of America

Editing: Lynda Exley
Cover and interior design: Linda Longmire

A Division of Five Star Publications, Inc.

What others are saying about
My Bonus Mom!

"Tami has thoughtfully and directly dealt with a topic generally associated with negative stereotypes in our society. While her words should be recommended reading to children involved in stepfamily situations, they are of equal importance to the adults involved, as well. This book shows a combined family is not about making a choice of one or the other, rather it is an opportunity filled with endless positive possibilities. 'The best interests of the children' is a frequent phrase in the world of divorce and stepfamilies. Tami successfully provides a road map with potential positive long-term effects for a child and family."

–Tim Mead, *V.P. LA Angels of Anaheim*

"My Bonus Mom! is not only a positive message for children who are experiencing the loss of their once intact family but it also sends a message to divorcing parents on how to 'do' divorce the right way. So many times children are not given the honest communication they need during the divorce process, causing confusion and fear. Thank you, Tami, for giving us this wonderful gift!"

–Dia Mundle, *LCSW, High School Social Worker*

"In this world of so many parents divorcing and remarrying, this book is delightfully positive for stepparents and will be an asset in the world of stepfamilies as well as in a therapeutic setting."

–Kim McDonald, *LMSW, LISAC*

Dedication

Bonus mom, Nancy Jefferies, Tami Butcher and mom, Candice Nagel

This book is dedicated to my mom, Candice, and my "Bonus Mom," Nancy. Both had a huge part in making me the person I am today. They were both the inspiration for this book and I will forever be grateful to them for putting their own egos aside to make life happier and easier for me and my three sisters. I love you both to the moon and back.

Foreword

Bill Engvall with his family – Travis, Emily and wife Gail.

I read Ms. Butcher's book and being a child of a divorce and remarriage I loved it.

Her book beautifully captures the stepparent and how he/she can be a wonderful added gift to a family. It is a great way to dispel the "evil stepmother" label that has been drilled into our society by old fairytales. Thank you, Ms. Butcher, for shedding a positive light on a situation that all too often has a bad reputation.

I love my stepmom. She did a great job of stepping into a difficult situation, and I would highly recommend any parent going through a similar situation to read this book to their child. Not only is it a cute read, but it is also written in a loving way that children can relate to. I wish this book had been around for me when I was a child going through divorce and remarriage. Well done, my friend, well done.

–Bill Engvall, *Comedian, television star of "The Bill Engvall Show" and "Blue Collar Comedy Tour"*

Acknowledgements

Diana Wright Kafka

My heartfelt thanks to everyone who helped bring this book to life, with special thanks to my family for always encouraging me to write. To my husband, Mike, for believing in everything that I do and always challenging me to dream big. To my children, Madison, Tatum and Brooks for being the light of my life. To my sisters for being my best friends and living this story with me. To my girlfriends, Leslee and Leslie for being the first to tell me I had written something very special, and to all the friends who have given me ideas, support, and words of advice. I would also like to thank Kari for giving me my first books about publishing, she obviously had faith! And finally, I would like to thank Linda and the Five Star team for believing in this book and being both a publisher and a friend.

Introduction

Candice Nagel

My Bonus Mom! is designed to provoke and inspire new thinking and speaking about stepparents. Why are they not "bonus parents?" Whoever said "sticks and stones can break my bones but words can never hurt me," did not understand just how powerful everyday words can be – especially to children. I cannot imagine calling Tami's "other mother" anything other than a BONUS! As parents, we hold the emotional life of our child in our hands. We need to put aside our own ego and start thinking about what we say and do, and how it affects children for the rest of their lives. Just rephrasing a term used for another person (like them or not) and just watch how differently they are perceived. Yes, Tami is my daughter; and yes, I am proud of the way she can turn a phrase. However, this book should be read to and by every child, parent, therapist and teacher when they have to deal with the emotions, and often the heartbreak, of a divorce and insecurities of a remarriage. Instead of children feeling like they are LOSING, they can think they are GAINING a bigger and better family. The commitment we made to hold the children first has enriched our lives, as well as theirs–tenfold! Please pass it on.

–Candice Nagel

Mother to the author, restaurant owner, former school board member, former Arizona State Legislator

My Bonus Mom!

Taking the Step out of Stepmom

WRITTEN BY:

Tami Butcher

•

ILLUSTRATED BY:

Feras Nouf

•

FOREWORD BY:

Bill Engvall

Almost eleven,
I remember it well
What seemed a sad story
Turned out really swell.

I felt kind of angry
I felt really sad,
What was the trouble
With Mom and with Dad?

One night in my bedroom
They sat us girls down
Talked about something
That made us all frown.

Daddy was leaving
He got a new house
I sat there and listened
Quiet as a mouse.

Did we do something bad
That made them both mad?
"Absolutely not!"
Said my Mom and my Dad.

7

Sometimes Mons and Dads
Just can't get along
But it's nothing about
The kids doing wrong.

And IT was decided
They called it DIVORCE
Our old way of life
Completely changed course.

On Mondays and Tuesdays
Mom's dinners were good
On Thursdays and Fridays
Dad made what he could.

EVery other weekend
We switched where we'd stay
Made sure that we talked
To both parents each day.

And then there were birthdays
They always came twice
One at Mom's, one at Dad's
Boy that sure was nice!

Holiday presents
Thanksgiving Day
Two of them all
Hip Hip Hooray!

About a year later
Dad met this girl
Her hair's not like Mom's
It was brown
and it curled.

We all sat so meekly
Looked her up, looked her down
No way can this lady
Be sticking around!

I asked where she lived
Which song topped her list?
Did she like scary movies?
Isn't Bieber the best?

Was Daddy her boyfriend?
Did she have any pets?
Were all of these questions
Making her feel upset?

19

She told me tomorrow
We'd go to the zoo
I could ask her more questions
It'd just be us two.

We spent the day talking
We laughed and we played
Ate lunch on a blanket
By a tree in the shade.

We looked at the monkeys
Saw a baby kangaroo
She told me the lions
Were her favorite, too.

The day went by quickly
And soon it would end
I felt very happy
I'd made a new friend.

I came home to Daddy
With a smile ear to ear
"How was your day?
I'd really love to hear."

"Nancy's the greatest
She really is smart
She loved all my stories
Did you know she likes art?"

From that day forward
She was always around
Family vacations
Trips out of town.

Mom even liked her
Said she's perfect for us
Loving, kind-hearted
And someone she trusts!

Snow skiing in Pinetop

One day in the Spring

Dad told us girls

He bought

Nancy a ring!

A wedding is coming
And what did we think?
Did this make us happy?
Or did it all stink?

She won't replace Mommy
But she'll be my wife
Let's call it a "Bonus"
That she's in our life.

I looked in Dad's eyes
And said so sincere
"I've got something to say,
So please listen here."

"You know I love Mommy
There's no one like her
She knows all my secrets
And loves me for sure!"

"**But** Nancy's a gift
Like winning a prize,
A 'Bonus Mom'
In all of our eyes."

And so a year later
At a wedding in spring
Dad married Nancy
And asked me to sing.

It's been 25 years
Since they exchanged vows
I have kids of my own
3, 6 and 10 now.

They don't know the difference
Between "bonus" and "real"
They only know "Grandma"
And the love that they feel.

So this is my story
And all of it's true
May you get a "Bonus"
In your lives too!

We all are so lucky
To DOUBLE our love
Someone is watching
From way up above!

And at the end of the day
If you think it all through
Bonus Moms, Bonus Dads
Means more love for YOU!

The End

About the Author

Tami Butcher

Tami Butcher made it her goal to write a children's book while teaching seventh-graders at Phoenix Prep Academy.

As a child, she grew up with what she lovingly refers to as her "bonus mom," a nurturing, caring woman many would refer to as a "stepmother." Butcher's parents amicably divorced when she was 11, and for the sake of Butcher and her three sisters, decided to keep each other fully involved in their children's lives despite the divorce. Eventually both her parents remarried, but they continued to share birthdays, holidays and special times together with their children, as well as with their new spouses. Because of her parents' efforts, Butcher and her sisters grew up feeling blessed for having two moms and dads instead of "stepparents."

Reflecting on her own family dynamics, Butcher realized that if she could plant a seed in children's minds that having a stepmother or stepfather can be a "bonus," then their minds and hearts might grow to accept their parents' new spouses instead of automatically thinking of them as evil as many childhood fairytales portray them. The product of that revelation was *My Bonus Mom!*

Currently, Butcher resides in Chandler, Ariz. with her husband and three children. When she's not volunteering, writing or promoting her new book, she helps with the family restaurant business. Her mother and "bonus dad" own Rustler's Rooste Steakhouse and Aunt Chilada's at Squaw Peak restaurants. Although her professional life is full, she always makes room for her greatest pride and joy: her family.

About Five Star

Tim Trimble

Linda Radke

Linda F. Radke, veteran publisher and owner of Five Star Publications, has been ahead of her game since 1985—self-publishing before it was commonplace, partnership publishing before the rest of the world even knew what it was, and producing award-winning traditionally and nontraditionally published fiction and nonfiction for adults and children.

Five Star Publications produces premium quality books for clients and authors. Many have been recognized for excellence on local, national and international levels.

Linda also is the author of *The Economical Guide to Self-Publishing* (a 2010 Paris Book Festival first-place winner in the "How-To" category and a Writer's Digest Book Club selection, now into its second edition) and *Promote Like a Pro: Small Budget, Big Show* (a Doubleday Executive Program Book Club selection). She is a founding member of the Arizona Book Publishing Association, was named "Book Marketer of the Year" by Book Publicists of Southern California, and received numerous public relations and marketing awards from Arizona Press Women.

Five Star Publications dedicates a percentage of profits to The Mark Foster Youth Fund and other charities chosen by the authors.

For more information about Five Star Publications, the Mark Foster Youth Fund, or charities supported by Five Star authors, visit www.FiveStarPublications.com.

My Bonus Mom!
Taking the Step out of Stepmom

"This is an excellent way to show children, through the eyes of the author, that they can have a great relationship with a new stepmother without being disloyal to Mom, and that divorces are not the fault of the children"

––-Tom Horne, Arizona State Attorney General

www.MyBonusMomBook.com

Order Form

ITEM	QTY	Unit Price	TOTAL
My Bonus Mom! Taking the Step out of Stepmom		$16.95 US $17.95 CAN	
▶▶▶▶▶▶▶▶▶▶▶▶▶▶▶▶▶▶▶▶ Subtotal			
* 8.8% sales tax – on all orders originating in Arizona.		*Tax	
$6.50 for the first book and $1.00 for each additional book going to the same address. (US rates) Ground shipping only. Allow 1 to 2 weeks for delivery.		*Shipping	
Mail form to: Five Star Publications, PO Box 6698, Chandler, AZ 85246-6698		TOTAL	

NAME:

ADDRESS:

CITY, STATE, ZIP:

DAYTIME PHONE: FAX:

EMAIL:

Method of Payment:
❑VISA ❑Master Card ❑Discover Card ❑American Express

account number   expiration date

signature   3-4 digit security number

❑ Yes, please send me a Five Star Publications catalog.
❑ Send me info about the author speaking at my event.
How were you referred to Five Star Publications?
❑ Friend ❑ Internet ❑ Book Show ❑ Other

P.O. Box 6698 • Chandler, AZ 85246-6698
(480) 940-8182   866-471-0777 Fax: (480) 940-8787
info@FiveStarPublications.com www.FiveStarPublications.com